SO-DTF-402

Red Wagon

RED WAGON

Ted Berrigan

The Yellow Press

Chicago

I am grateful to the editors who printed many of these
poems in their magazines, to Tom Clark who used some
of the poems in *All*Stars*, and to Bob Rosenthal &
Rochelle Kraut who first printed some of these poems in
my book *A Feeling For Leaving*, Frontward Books, NYC.

Cover by Rochelle Kraut

Back Photograph by Gerard Malanga

Library of Congress Cataloging in Publication Data

Berrigan, Ted.
    Red wagon.

    I. Title.
PS3552.E74R4   811'.5'4   76-26054
ISBN 0-916328-05-8
ISBN 0-916328-01-5 pbk.

Yellow Press books are distributed by
Serendipity Books 1790 Shattuck Avenue
Berkeley, Ca 94709
Address all orders to them

The Yellow Press
2394 Blue Island
Chicago, Il 60608

Publication of this book was partially supported by
a grant from The National Endowment for The Arts.

To Alice Notley

SHE

She is always two blue eyes
She is never lost in sleep
All her dreams are light & air
They sometimes melt the sun
She makes me smile, or
She makes me cry, she
Makes me laugh, and I talk to her
With really nothing particularly to say.

REMEMBERED POEM

It is important to keep old hat
in secret closet.

3 PAGES

for Jack Collom

10 Things I do Every Day

            play poker
            drink beer
            smoke pot
            jack off
    curse

BY THE WATERS OF MANHATTAN

                        flower

    positive & negative

go home

            read   lunch   poems

            hunker down

        changes

                Life goes by
                        quite merrily
                                                blue
                NO HELP WANTED

                        Hunting For The Whale

            "and if the weather plays me fair
            I'm happy every day."

            The white that dries clear
            the heart attack
            the congressional medal of honor
            A house in the country

            NOT ENOUGH

CONVERSATION

"My name
"My name   "My name
"My name   "My name
"My name   is Wesley
is Wesley   Wesley
is Wesley   Jackson,
is Wesley Jackson, "My name is Wesley Jackson,
I am   I am
I am   I am
25 years   25 years
old,   old,
I am 25 years old, I am 25 years old,
I am 25 years old, and
and   my favorite
my favorite   my favorite
favorite   favorite
and my favorite   song
song   song
and my favorite   and my favorite song
and my favorite song my favorite song
and my favorite song is
is *Valencia*."   *Valencia*."

"Isn't
"Isn't   that
"Isn't that   beautiful,"
beautiful,"   "Isn't that beautiful,"
"Isn't that beautiful," Frank
Frank   said.
Frank said.

TO SOUTHAMPTON

Go
Get in Volkswagen
Ride to the Atlantic
Step out
See
Your shadows
On fog

At the second stop
The same ocean as
At the first

Back in Volkswagen
Ron's or somebody's
Backs up
Steps on the gas

COCA COLA 20 Cents

Machine noise

Satisfaction

Home
Away from home.

SUNDAY MORNING

for Lou Reed

1.

It's A Fact

If you stroke a cat about 1,000,000 times, you will
generate enough electricity to light up the largest
American Flag in the world for about one minute.

2.

Turnabout

In former times people who committed adultery
            got stoned;
Nowadays it's just a crashing bringdown.

3.

A Mongolian Sausage

By definition: a long stocking: you fill it full of shit,
and then you punch holes in it. Then you swing it over
your head in circles until everybody goes home.

SOMETHING AMAZING JUST HAPPENED

for Jim Carroll, on his birthday

A lovely body gracefully is nodding
Out of a blue Buffalo
                    Monday morning
                                curls
softly rising color the air
                    it's yellow
above the black plane
                    beneath a red tensor

I've been dreaming. The telephone kept ringing & ringing
Clear & direct, purposeful yet pleasant, still taking pleasure
in bringing the good news, a young man in horn-rims' voice
                                        is speaking
while I listen. Mr. Berrigan, he says, & without waiting for an answer
        goes on,
I'm happy to be able to inform you that your request for a Guggenheim
        Foundation Grant
Has been favorably received by the committee, & approved. When
        would you like to leave?

Uh, not just yet, I said, uh, what exactly did I say with regards to leaving,
        in my application... I'm a little hazy at the moment.

Yes. Your project, as outlined in your application for a grant for the
        purpose
of giving Jim Carroll the best possible birthday present you could get
        him, through our Foundation, actually left the project, that is,
        how the monies
would be spent, up to us. You indicated, wisely, I think, that we knew
        more about what kind of project we would approve than you did,
        so we should
make one up for you, since all you wanted was money, to buy Jim a
        birthday gift.

Aha! I said. So, what's up?

We have arranged for you and Jim to spend a year in London, in a flat
        off of King's Row.
You will receive 250 pounds each a month expenses, all travel expenses

paid, & a clothing allowance of 25 pounds each per month.
During the year,
At your leisure, you might send us from time to time copies of your
London works. By year's end I'm sure you each will have enough
new poems for two books,
Which we would then publish in a deluxe boxed hardcover edition, for
the rights to which we shall be prepared to pay a considerable
sum, as is your due.
We feel that this inspired project will most surely result in The first major
boxed set of works since Tom Sawyer & Huckleberry Finn!
Innocents Abroad
in reverse, so to speak! We know your poems, yours & Jim's, will tell it
like it is, & that is what we are desperate to know! So, when
would you like to leave?
Immediately, I shouted! & Jim! I called, Jim! Happy Birthday! Wake up!

TODAY IN ANN ARBOR

for Jayne Nodland

Today I woke up
              bright & early

Then I went back to sleep

              I had a nice dream
         which left me weak
                        so
         I woke up again
                   dull, but still early.

    I drank some coke
            & took a pill

         It made me feel ill, but

         optimistic. So,

    I went to the Michigan Union for cigarettes.

                  *

I cashed a check today—
                  but that was later. Now
         I bought cigarettes, &
                        The Detroit Free Press.

    I decided to eat some vanilla wafers
            & drink coffee
                   at my desk

              *

         There was no cream for
            the coffee. & the mail
            wasn't out yet.

               It pissed me off.

9

I drank some coffee, black
& it was horrible.

*

Life is horrible, &

I am stupid.

I think..........NOTHING.

Then I think, more coffee...
                                upstairs!

                        Jackie's face
                                picks me up.

        She says,   "there's cream
                            upstairs"

            Up more stairs via the elevator:

        cream   talk amiably to Bert
                            Hornbach

                    *

Come downstairs
                        &
                            the mail has
                            come!
            Lots
            of mail!   I feel pretty good.

    Together with my mail back in office.

                                Sitting.

            *

Johnny Stanton says: "Ted,

    you are a myth in my heart."

He is a myth in my heart!

So, we are both myths!

*

Warmed by this, & coffee,

  I go on. American Express
        says:

        "You owe us $1,906. Please

          Pay *NOW*."

    I say, *sure!*

  ("Now" means "later")

    *

Somebody else sends a postcard (Bill).

    He says,

      "I am advertising your presence
      at YALE, so please come!"

        I say to Bill,

      "Have Faith, old

        brother! I'll be there
           when you need me."

   In fact, I say that to everyone.

  That is the truth,

      & so,

    *

I open a beautiful letter

  from you. When we are both dead,

that letter
   will be Part Two
      of this poem.

    *

But now we are both alive

 & terrific!

IN THE WHEEL

The pregnant waitress
asks
      "Would you like
some more coffee?"
Surprised out of the question
I wait   seconds   "Yes,
I think I would!" I hand her
      my empty cup, &
"thank you!" she says. My pleasure.

WIND

Every day when the sun comes up
The angels emerge from the rivers
Drily happy & all wet. Easy going
But hard to keep my place. Easy
On the avenue underneath my face.
Difficult alone trying to get true.
Difficult inside alone with you.
The rivers' blackness flowing just sits
Orange & reds blaze up inside the sky
I sit here & I've been thinking this
Red, blue, yellow, green, & white.

THINGS TO DO ON SPEED

mind clicks into gear
& fingers clatter over the keyboard
as intricate insights stream
> out of your head:

> this goes on for ten hours:

> then, take a break: clean
> all desk drawers, arrange all
> pens & pencils in precise parallel patterns;
> stack all books with exactitude in one pile
> to coincide perfectly with the right angle
> of the desk's corner.

Whistle thru ten more hours of
arcane insights:
> drink a quart of ice-cold pepsi:
> clean the ice-box:
> > pass out for ten solid hours

> interesting dreams.

2.

Finish papers, wax floors, lose weight, write songs, sing songs, have
conference, sculpt, wake up & think more clearly. Clear up asthma.

treat your obesity, avoid mild depression, decongest, cure your
        narcolepsy,
treat your hyper-kinetic brain-damaged children. Open the Pandora's Box

of amphetamine abuse.

3.

Stretch the emotional sine curve; follow euphoric peaks with descents

into troughs
that are unbearable wells of despair & depression. Become a ravaged
   scarecrow.

Cock your emaciated body in
twisted postures   grind your caved-in jaw

                    scratch your torn & pock-marked skin,
                    keep talking, endlessly.

                         4.

Jump off a roof on the lower East Side

                    or

                    Write a 453 page unintelligible book

                    5.

Dismantle 12 radios

                         string beads interminably

         empty your purse

                         sit curled in a chair
                         & draw intricate designs
                            in the corner of an envelope

                    6.

"I felt it rush almost instantly into
my head like a short circuit. My body
began to pulsate, & grew tiny antennae
all quivering in anticipation. I began
to receive telepathic communication from
the people around me. I felt elated."

get pissed off.

> Feel your tongue begin to shred,
> lips to crack, the inside of the mouth
> become eaten out. Itch all over. See
> your fingernails flake off, hair & teeth
> fall out.

Buy a Rolls-Royce

Become chief of the Mafia

Consider anti-matter.

8.

Notice that tiny bugs are crawling over your whole body
around, between and over your many new pimples.

> Cut away pieces of bad flesh.

Discuss mother's promiscuity

Sense the presence of danger at the movies

Reveal

> get tough

> turn queer

9.

In the Winter, switch to heroin, so you won't catch pneumonia.

In the Spring, go back to speed.

TELEVISION

San Gabriel
Placer, Nevada. New York:
Buffalo. 24 Huntington, just off of Main.
$12.95 takes you
                        where you want to go
quick; & quickly do you go.
$.30 will bring you back
sweating, worn out. Twice
as fast (as when you went) is
slow.

FAREWELL ADDRESS

to Richard Taylor

Goodbye House, 24 Huntington, one block past Hertel
   on the downtown side of Main, second house on the left.
   Your good spirit kept me cool this summer, your ample space.
Goodbye house.

Goodbye our room, on the third floor. Your beds were much appreciated;
   We used them gratefully & well, me & Alice. & Alice's yellow blanket
   spread across to the yellow slanted ceiling to make a lovely light,
   Buffalo mornings. There we talked, O did we ever! Goodbye, our
Third floor room.

& Goodbye other room across the hall. Typewriter music filled my heart.
   Buffalo nights as I read on my bed while Alice wrote unseen. Her
   Buffalo poems were terrific, & they were even about me! Some
   had you in them, too! So,
Goodbye room.

Goodbye second floor. Your bathroom's character one could grow to
   understand. I liked the sexy closed door of Chris's room, &
   light showing under the master's door at night; a good omen to me,
   always! Even your unused office offered us its ironing board, by
   moonlight.
You were friendly. Goodbye second floor of Richard's house.

Goodbye stairs. Alice knew you well.

& Goodbye first floor. Goodbye kitchen, you were a delight; you
   fed us morning, noon & night; I liked your weird yellow light, &
   your wall clock was out of sight! Meals we shared with Richard
   were gentle & polite; we liked them; we liked those times a lot.
Goodbye kitchen, you'll not be forgot.

& Goodbye Arboretum. (I mean TV room) Mornings, alone, I loved to sit
   in you, to read the news from the world of sports, as light
   poured into & through the house. Mornings were quiet pepsis.
   Nights I'd talk with Richard over beers. Good manners had some

meaning here; I learned better ones with great delight. Goodbye
TV room. Thanks for your mornings and nights.

Goodbye vast dining hall, where we three & three dogs often ate
of beef & drank red wine. Your table was long, & your chandelier
a sight. Richard ate quickly, as did Alice, while I took my time,
talking beneath your light. May we dine thusly many a night, days
To come. Goodbye dining room, & dogs who ate our bones with delight.

Goodbye Thelonius. Only Allen Ginsberg, for beauty, matches you. &
Goodbye Ishmael. I liked your ghastly rough-house ways. You
were the love/hate delight of Alice's days & nights. Many a fond
lick you lolled her way, each of her trips. Goodbye Ishmael.
Goodbye Oliver. You didn't say much, but you were always there,
calling "Hey, wait for me!" like in those movies I used to like
the best. When you three ate Bobby Dylan's SELF PORTRAIT, it
put our friendship to the test. But it survived. & so,
Goodbye Ishmael, Thelonius, Oliver; friends, my brothers, dogs.

& Richard, goodbye, too, to you. You were the best of all our Buffalo
life. Sharing with you made it *be* a life. We were at home in
your house, because it's yours. It was a great pleasure, to come & go
through your doors. Nothing gets lost, in anyone's life;
I'm glad of that. We three had our summer, which will last. Poems
last (like this one has); and so do memories. They last in poems,
& in the people in them (who are us). So, although this morning
under the sky, we go, Alice & I, you'll be flying with us as we fly.
You come to visit, where we go, & we'll sometimes visit you in
Buffalo. Bring the dogs, too. & until then, our love to you, Richard.

Goodbye.

THREE SONNETS AND A CODA FOR TOM CLARK

1.

In The Early Morning Rain
To my family & friends   "Hello"
And money. With something inside us we float up
On this electric chair each breath nearer the last
Now is spinning
Seven thousand feet over / The American Midwest
Gus walked up under the arc light as far as the first person
the part that goes over the fence last
And down into a green forest ravine   near to "her"
Winds in the stratosphere
                          Apologise to the malcontents
Downstairs. The black bag & the wise man may be found
        in the brain-room.
what sky out there   Take it away
                  & it's off
one foot
            is expressing itself as continuum
the other, sock

2.

Tomorrow.   I need to kill
Blank mind part   Confusions of the cloth
White snow whirls everywhere.   Across the fields
in the sky the
            Soft, loose
stars swarm. Nature makes my teeth "to hurt"
shivering now   on 32nd Street   in my face & in my head
does Bobby Dylan ever come around here?   listen
it's alive   where exposed nerve jangles
& I   looming over Jap's American flag
In Public, In Private   The Sky Pilot In No Man's Land
The World Number 14   is tipsy as pinballs on the ocean
We are bored through.....through.....with our professionalism
Outside her
Windows

3

I'm amazed to be here
A man who can do the average thing
                                    when everybody else is
going crazy   Lord I wonder just exactly what can happen
my heart is filled (filling)   with light
& there's a breeze   & I'm going
                                way over
the white   skyline   do what I want to
Fuck it.
                        Tied up wit
Tie with red roses   The war of the Roses, &
War is shit.   White man, tomorrow you die!
Tomorrow means *now*.   "You kidding me?" now.
Light up   you will be great
It's a complication.   Thanksgiving, 1970, Fall.

CODA:

Being a new day my heart
is confirmed in its pure Buddhahood
activity under the clear blue sky
The front is hiding the rear (not)
which means we have (not) "protected ourselves"
by forgetting all we were dealt
I love all the nuts I've been in bed (with)
hope to go everywhere in good time
like, Africa: it would be tremendous (or not)
to drink up rivers. Be seeing *you*
to ride the river (with)   heads riding gently
its personal place   feet doing their stuff   up in the air
Where someone (J.) dies, so that we can be rude to friends
While you find me right here coming through again.

LANDSCAPE WITH FIGURES (SOUTHAMPTON)

There's a strange lady in my front yard
She's wearing blue slacks & a white car-coat
& "C'mon!" she's snarling at a little boy
He isn't old enough to snarl, so he's whining
On the string as first she & then he disappear
Into (or is it behind) the Rivers' garage.
                                    That's 11 a.m.
In the country. "Everything is really golden,"
Alice, in bed, says. I look, & out the window, see
Three shades of green; & the sky, not so high,
So blue & white. "You're right, it really is!"

WHAT I'D LIKE FOR CHRISTMAS, 1970

Black brothers to get happy

The Puerto Ricans to say hello

The old folks to take it easy &

                                     as it comes

The United States to get straight

Power to butt out

Money to fuck off

Business with honor

Religion

                &

Art

Love

A home

A typewriter

A GUN.

LADY

Nancy, Jimmy, Larry, Frank, & Berdie
George & Bill
    Dagwood Bumstead
         Donna, Joe, & Phil
Making shapes this place
      so rightly ours
         to fill
as we wish,
   & Andy's flowers too, do.

    *

    I've been sitting, looking
thinking sounds of pictures
      names
       of you

    *

  of how I smile now

   &

    Let It Be.

    *

& now I think to add
     "steel teeth"
           "sucking cigarette"
  "A photograph of Bad."

    Everything you are gone slightly mad.
  America.

36TH BIRTHDAY AFTERNOON

Green TIDE; behind, pink against blue
Blue CHEER; an expectorant, *Moving On*
Gun in hand, shooting down
Anyone who comes to mind

IN OLD SOUTHAMPTON, blue, shooting up
THE SCRIPTURE OF THE GOLDEN ETERNITY
A new sharpness, peel apart to open, bloody water
& Alice is putting her panties on, taking off

A flowery dress for London's purple one
It seems to be getting longer, the robot
Keeps punching, opening up
A bit at a time. Up above

Spread atop the bed a red head sees
Two hands, one writing, one holding on.

TODAY'S NEWS

My body heavy with poverty (starch)
It uses up my sexual energy
      constantly, &
I feel constantly crowded

On the other hand, *One
Day In The Afternoon of
    The World*
Pervaded my life with a
    heavy grace
             today

I'll never smile again

Bad Teeth

But
I'm dancing with tears in my eyes
(I can't help myself!)   Tom
writes he loves Alice's sonnets,
    takes four, I'd love

to be more attentive to her, more
    here.
The situation having become intolerable
the only alternatives are:
    Murder & Suicide.

They are too dumb! So, one
becomes a goof. Raindrops
start falling on my roof. I say
Hooray! Then I say, I'm going out

At the drugstore I say, Gimme some pills!
    Charge 'em! They say
Sure. I say See you later.

Read the paper. Talk to Alice.
She laughs to hear
   Hokusai had 947 changes of address
In his life. Ha-ha. Plus everything
   else in the world
going on here.

WISHES

Now I wish I were asleep, to see my dreams taking place
I wish I were more awake
I wish a sweet rush of tears to my eyes
Wish a nose like an eagle
I wish blue sky in the afternoon
Bigger windows, & a panorama—light, buildings & people in street air
Wish my teeth were white and sparkled
Wish my legs were not where they are—where they are
I wish the days warmly cool & clothes I like to be inside of
Wish I were walking around in Chelsea (NY) & it was 5:15 a.m., the
    sun coming up, alone, you asleep at home
I wish red rage came easier
I wish death, but not just now
I wish I were driving alone across America in a gold Cadillac
    toward California, & my best friend
I wish I were in love, & you here

OPHELIA

                    ripped
                        out of her mind

        a marvelous construction

            thinking

                        no place; & you
                        not once properly handled

        Ophelia

            &

        you can't handle yourself
                                feeling
                            no inclination
                        toward that
                                solitude,
                                        love
                            by yourself

                        Ophelia

            & feeling free   you drift

                far more beautifully
                                    than we

        As one now understands

    He never did see   you

            you moving so   while talking flashed
                                    & failed
                                        to let you go

                        Ophelia

SCORPION, EAGLE & DOVE (A LOVE POEM)

for Pat

November, dancing, or
Going to the store in the country,
Where green changes itself into LIFE,
MOVING ON, Jockey Shorts, Katzenmiaou
A Chesterfield King & the blue book
IN OLD SOUTHAMPTON,
                              you make my days special

You do Jimmy's, & Alice's,
Phoebe's, Linda's,
                    Lewis' & Joanne's, too. . .
& Kathy's (a friend who is new) . . .

& Gram's . . .
            who loved you,
                            like I do
            once . . .

& who surely does so since
                    that 4th of July last,
a Saturday,
            a day that left her free
to be with & love you
                    (& me)
                            (all of us)
just purely;
            clean;
                    & selflessly;

                    *

        no thoughts

                    *

Just, It's true. As I would be
& as I am, to you
                    this
                            November.

31

THINGS TO DO IN PROVIDENCE

Crash

Take Valium   Sleep

Dream &,

forget it.

*

Wake up new & strange

displaced,

at home.

Read The Providence Evening Bulletin

No one you knew

got married
had children
got divorced
died

got born

tho many familiar names flicker &
disappear.

*

Sit

watch TV

draw blanks

32

swallow

>> pepsi
>> meatballs
>> ...

>>>> give yourself the needle:

>> "Shit! There's gotta be something
>>>> to do
>>>>> here!"

*

JOURNEY TO   Seven young men on horses, leaving Texas.
SHILOH: They've got to do what's right! So, after
             a long trip, they'll fight for the South in the War.
             No war in Texas, but they've heard about it, & they want
             to fight for their country. Have some adventures & make
             their folks proud! Two hours later all are dead;
             one by one they died, stupidly, & they never did find out
             why! There were no niggers in South Texas! Only
                     the leader,
             with one arm shot off, survives to head back for Texas:
             all his friends behind him, dead. What will happen?

*

>> Watching him, I cry big tears. His friends
> were beautiful, with boyish American good manners,
>>>> cowboys!

*

Telephone New York: "hello!"

>>>> "Hello! I'm drunk! &
>>>>> I have no clothes on!"

33

"My goodness," I say.

"See you tomorrow."

*

Wide awake all night reading: *The Life of Turner*
("He first saw the light in Maiden Lane")
A.C. Becker: Wholesale Jewels
Catalogue 1912
The Book of Marvels, 1934:
The year I was born.

No mention of my birth in here.   Hmmm.

Saturday The Rabbi Stayed Home

(that way he got to solve the murder)

LIFE on the Moon   by LIFE Magazine.

*

My mother wakes up, 4 a.m.: Someone to talk with!

Over coffee we chat, two grownups
I have two children, I'm an adult now, too.
Now we are two people talking who have known each other
a long time,
Like Edwin & Rudy. Our talk is a great pleasure: my mother
a spunky woman. Her name was Peggy Dugan when she was young.
Now, 61 years old, she blushes to tell me I was conceived
before the wedding! "I've always been embarrassed about telling you
til now," she says. "I didn't know what you might think!"
"I think it's really sweet," I say. "It means I'm really
a love child." She too was conceived before her mother's wedding,
I know. We talk, daylight comes, & the Providence Morning Journal.
My mother leaves for work. I'm still here.

*

Put out the cat

                             Take in the clothes
                                   off of the line

                Take a walk,
                      buy cigarettes

          *

two teen-agers whistle
                as I walk up

                      They say: "Only your hairdresser
                              knows for sure!"

              Then they say,

                  "ulp!"

                because I am closer to them.
         They see I am not hippie kid, frail like Mick Jagger,
    but some horrible 35 year old big guy!

                    The neighborhood I live in is mine!

"How'd you like a broken head, kid?"
                        I say fiercely.

          (but I am laughing & they are not one bit scared.)

                So, I go home.

          ****

Alice Clifford waits me. Soon she'll die
at the Greenwood Nursing Home; my mother's
mother, 79 years & 7 months old.
                  But first, a nap, til my mother comes home
                  from work, with the car.

          *

The heart stops briefly when someone dies,
a quick pain as you hear the news, & someone passes
from your outside life to inside. Slowly the heart adjusts
to its new weight, & slowly everything continues, sanely.

*

Living's a pleasure:
                    I'd like to take the whole trip

            despite the possible indignities of growing old,
        moving, to die in poverty, among strangers:
                                    that can't be helped.

*

So, everything, now
        is just all right.   I'm with you.

            No more last night.

*

        Friday's great

        10 o'clock morning sun is shining!

        I can hear today's key sounds fading softly

        & almost see opening sleep's epic novels.

                * * * *

FRANK O'HARA

Winter in the country, Southampton, pale horse
as the soot rises, then settles, over the pictures
The birds that were singing this morning have shut up
I thought I saw a couple, kissing, but Larry said no
It's a strange bird. He should know. & I think now
"Grandmother divided by monkey equals outer space." Ron
put me in that picture. In another picture, a good-
looking poet is thinking it over; nevertheless, he will
never speak of that it. But, his face is open, his eyes
are clear, and, leaning lightly on an elbow, fist below
his ear, he will never be less than perfectly frank,
listening, completely interested in whatever there may
be to hear. Attentive to me alone here. Between friends,
nothing would seem stranger to me than true intimacy.
What seems genuine, truly real, is thinking of you, how
that makes me feel. You are dead. And you'll never
write again about the country, that's true.
But the people in the sky really love
to have dinner & to take a walk with you.

CRYSTAL

Be awake mornings. See light spread across the lawn
(snow) as the sky refuses to be any color, today
I like this boat-ride I'm being taken for, although
It never leaves the shore, this boat. Its fires burn
Like a pair of lovely legs. It's a garage that grew up
Sometimes I can't talk, my mouth too full of words, but
I have hands & other parts, to talk lots! Light the fire
Babble for you. I dream a green undersea man
Has been assigned to me, to keep me company, to smirk
At me when I am being foolish. A not unpleasant dream.
My secret doors open as the mail arrives. Fresh air
Pours in, around, before they close again. The winds are rushing
Up off of the ocean, up Little Plains Road. Catch the Wind
In my head, a quiet song. And, "Everything belongs to me
Because I am poor." Waiting in sexy silence, someone
Turns over in bed, & waiting is just a way of being with
Now a tiny fire flares out front the fireplace. Chesterfield
King lights up! Wood is crackling inside
Elephants' rush & roar. Refrigerator's gentle drone
Imagined footsteps moving towards my door. Sounds in dreams
In bed. You are all there is inside my head.

CLOWN

There's a strange lady in my front yard
A girl naked in the shower, saying
"I'm keeping my boxes dry!" A naked artist
Smoking. Bad teeth. Wooden planks: furniture. Sky
One minute ago I stopped thought: 12 years of cops
In my life. & Alice is putting her panties on
Takes off a flowery dress for London's purple one
Out of the blue, a host of words, floating
March: awaiting rescue: smoke, or don't
Strapped: deprived. Shoot yourself: stay alive.
& you can't handle yourself, love, feeling
No inclination toward that solitude.
Take it easy, & as it comes. Coffee
Suss. Feel. Whine. *Shut up.* Exercise.
Turn. Turn around. Turn. *Kill dog.*
Today woke up bright & early, no mail, life
Is horrible, & I am stupid, & I think.....Nothing.
"Have faith, old brother. You are a myth in my heart.
We are both alive. Today we may go to India."

CHINESE NIGHTINGALE

We are involved in a transpersonified state
Revolution, which is turning yourself around
I am asleep next to "The Hulk." "The Hulk" often sleeps
While I am awake & vice versa. Life is less than ideal
For a monkey in love with a nymphomaniac! God is fired!
Do I need the moon to remain free? To explode softly
In a halo of moon rays? Do I need to be
On my human feet, straight, talking, free
Will sleep cure the deaf-mute's heartbreak? Am I
In my own way, America? Rolling downhill, & away?
The door to the river is closed, my heart is breaking
Loose from sheer inertia. All I do is bumble. No
Matter. We live together in the jungle.

WRONG TRAIN

Here comes the man! He's talking a lot
I'm sitting, by myself. I've got
A ticket to ride. Outside is, "Out to Lunch."
It's no great pleasure, being on the make.
Well, who is? Or, well everyone is, tho.
"I'm laying there, & some guy comes up
& hits me with a billyclub!" A fat guy
Says. Shut up. & like that we cross a river
Into the Afterlife. Everything goes on as before
But never does any single experience make total use
Of you. You are always slightly ahead,
Slightly behind. It merely baffles, it doesn't hurt.
It's total pain & it breaks your heart
In a less than interesting way. Every day
Is payday. Never enough pay. A deja-vu
That lasts. It's no big thing, anyway.
A lukewarm greasy hamburger, ice-cold pepsi
        that hurts your teeth.

BUDDHA ON THE BOUNTY

"A little loving can solve a lot of things"
She locates two spatial equivalents in
The same time continuum. "You are lovely. I
am lame." "Now it's me." "If a man is in
Solitude, the world is translated, my world
& wings sprout from the shoulders of 'The Slave'"
Yeah. I like the fiery butterfly puzzles
Of this pilgrimage toward clarities
Of great mud intelligence & feeling.
"The Elephant is the wisest of all animals
The only one who remembers his former lives
& he remains motionless for long periods of time
Meditating thereon." I'm not here, now,
      & it is good, absence.

SCORPIO

If I don't love you I
Won't let it show. But I'll
Make it clear, by
Never letting you know.

& if I love you, I will
Love you true: insofar
As Love, itself,
Will do.

& while I live, I'll be
Whatever I am, whose
Constant, impure, fire
Is outwardly only a man.

I USED TO BE BUT NOW I AM

I used to be inexorable,
But now I am elusive.

I used to be the future of America,
But now I am America.

I used to be part of the problem,
But now I am the problem.

I used to be part of the solution, if not all of it,
But now I am not that person.

I used to be intense, & useful,
But now I am heavy, & boring.

I used to be sentimental about myself, & therefore ruthless,
But now I am, I think, a sympathetic person, although
        easily amused.

I used to be a believer,
But now, alas, I believe.

OLD-FASHIONED AIR

to Lee Crabtree

I'm living in Battersea, July,
1973, not sleeping, reading
Jet noise throbs building fading
Into baby talking, no, "speechifying"
"Ah wob chuk sh'guh!" Glee.
There's a famous Power Station I can't see
Up the street. Across there is
Battersea Park
I walked across this morning toward
A truly gorgeous radiant flush;
Sun; fumes of the Battersea
Power Station; London Air;
I walked down long avenues with trees
That leant not ungracefully
Over the concrete walk. Wet green lawn
Opened spaciously
Out on either side of me. I saw
A great flock of geese taking their morning walk
Unhurriedly.
I didn't hurry either, Lee.
I stopped & watched them walk back up toward
& down into their lake,
Smoked a Senior Service on a bench
As they swam past me in a long dumb graceful cluttered line,
Then, taking my time, I found my way
Out of that park:
A Gate that was locked. I jumped the fence.
From there I picked up the *London Times*, came home,
Anselm awake in his bed, Alice
Sleeping in mine: I changed
A diaper, read a small poem I'd had
In mind, then thought to write this line:
"Now is Monday morning so, that's a garbage truck I hear,
        not bells"...
And we are back where we started from, Lee, you
        & me, alive & well!"

CHICAGO MORNING

for Philip Guston

Under a red face, black velvet shyness
Milking an emaciated gaffer. God lies down
Here. Rattling of a shot engine, heard
From the first row. The president of the United States
And the Director of the FBI stand over
A dead mule. "Yes, it is nice to hear the fountain
With the green trees around it, as well as
People who need me." Quote Lovers of speech unquote. It's
            a nice thought
& typical of a rat. And, it is far more elaborate
Than expected. And the thing is, we don't *need*
            that much money.
Sunday morning; blues, blacks, red & yellow wander
In the soup. Grey in the windows' frames. The angular
Explosion in the hips. A huge camel rests
            in a massive hand
Casts clouds a smoggish white out & up over the Loop, while
Two factories (bricks) & a fortress of an oven (kiln)
Rise, barely visible inside a grey metallic gust.
            "The Fop's Tunic."
She gets down, off of the table, breaking a few more plates.
Natives paint their insides crystal white here (rooms)
Outside is more bricks, off-white. Europe at Night.

NEWTOWN

Sunday morning: here we live jostling & tricky
blues, blacks, reds & yellows all are gray
in each window: the urbanites have muscles
in their butts & backs; shy, rough, compassionate
& good natured, "they have sex in their pockets"
To women in love with my flesh I speak.
All the Irish major statements & half the best
Low-slung stone. Upstairs is sleep. Downstairs
is heat. She seems exceedingly thin and transparent
Two suspicious characters in my head. They park & then
Start, the same way you get out of bed. The pansy is
Grouchy. The Ideal Family awaits distribution on
The Planet. Another sensation tugged at his heart
Which he could not yet identify,
half Rumanian deathbed diamond
Wildly singing in the mountains with cancer of the spine.

THE END

Despair farms a curse, slackness
In the sleep of animals, with mangled limbs
Dogs, frogs, game elephants, while
There's your new life, blasted with milk.
It's the last day of summer, it's the first
Day of fall: soot sits on Chicago like
A fat head's hat. The quick abounds. Turn
To the left, turn to the right. On Bear's Head
Two Malted Milk balls. "Through not taking himself
Quietly enough he strained his insides." He
Encourages criticism, but he never forgives it.
You who are the class in the sky, receive him
Into where you dwell. May he rest long and well.
God help him, he invented us, that is, a future
Open living beneath his spell. One goes not where
One came from. One sitting says, "I stand corrected."

CHICAGO ENGLISH AFTERNOON

He never listened while friends talked
Less original than penetrating, very often
Illuminating   He worked steadily to the even
Current of sound   sunlit oblongs   bramble transfer
White South   nothing is gained by assurance as
To what is insecure   beer in bed, & an unused point
Beside me on the bench   time of, major energy product
Over Belle Vue Road that silence said
To mean angels are passing overhead   my baby
Throws my shoes out the door   & one cannot go back
Except in time   "Yes, but he is exultant; the ice
Meant something else to him"   highly reduced
For the sake of maintaining scale   *Goodbye To All That*
"I have only one work, & I hardly know what it is!"
It was silence that stopped him working, silence in which he might
        look up
& see terror waiting in their eyes for his attention.
"Ladies & Gentlemen, you will depart the aircraft
At the Terminal Area to your Right. Thank you for flying United."

FROM A LIST OF DELUSIONS OF THE INSANE
WHAT THEY ARE AFRAID OF

That they are starving.
That their blood has turned to water.
That they give off a bad smell.
Being poor.
That they are in hell.
That they are the tools of another power.
That they have stolen something.
That they have committed an unpardonable sin.
Being unfit to live.
That evil chemicals have entered the air.
Being ill with a mysterious disease.
That they will not recover.
That their children are burning.

LATE NOVEMBER

What said your light
you know, an answer refusing
I go to my store I maintain
animal inextricably between

illuminated, on the line
something lords in chair
all fixtured silvered
heart, your curtain, air

breathy air stirs white
knowing refusing running
Waitomo Cave New Zealand
couldn't catch the day, its curve, its more

Committed robbery with the Smothers Brothers
cops pursue us infinitely

QUARTER TO THREE

"who is not here
causes us to drift"

wake up, throat dry,
that way, perpetually,

"and why deprived unless
you feel that you ought to be?" and

"Clarity is immobile." And, "We are hungry
for devices to keep the baby happy. . ."

She writes, "My hunger creates a food
that everybody needs."

"I can't live without you, no
matter who you are." "I think."

I write this in cold blood,
        enjoy.

SHE (Not to be confused with she, a girl)

She alters all our lives for the better, merely
By her presence in it. She is a star. She is
Radiant, & She is vibrant (integrity). She animates
And gathers this community. Half the world's population
Is under 25. She permits everybody to be themselves more often
        than not.
She is elegant. I love her.
                     She writes poetry of an easy & graceful
Intimacy. She is brave. She is always slightly breathless, or
Almost always slightly. She is witty. She owns a proud & lovely
Dignity, & She is always willing to see it through.
She is an open circle, Her many selves at or near the center, &
She is here right now. Technically, she is impeccable, &
If She is clumsy in places, those are clumsy places. She knows
Exactly what she is doing & not before She is doing it. What
She discovers She discovered before She discovers it, and so
The fresh discovery of each new day. Her songs are joyous songs,
& they are prayers, never failing to catch the rush of hope
        (anticipation)
Despair, insanity, & desperation pouring in any given moment. She
Knows more than She will ever say. She will always say
More than she knows. She is a pain. She is much less than
Too good to be true. She is plain. She is ordinary. She
        is a miracle.

SISTER MOON

Where do the words come from? (come in?)
Where did that silt?   How much lives?
A rock is next to the bee.
The window is never totally thought through.
So
"Silver" is used to stand for something nothing
really ever quite is. Let it stand against.
Or in other words what next?   There's time enough
                                  for a list to occur
A lot of unalloyed nouns.   between the lines.
Weather, as all strata in a possible day.
Sleet against window glass. A cigarette starts sounding.
You can see how "a depth" makes "west" and "south" agree.
A philosophy: "I guess yes".
milks & honeys, stuns, salutes, flashes...
                              now & again, "a glimpse"

FOUR GATES TO THE CITY

Everything good is from the Indian
Sober dog, O expert caresses
By light that breathes like a hand
Small   immobile   yellow   yo-yo plumage
On the cold bomb-shelter. A cur
Is a pre-sound without a rage
Come with me the nurse ferocity
Whose clouds are really toots from the nearby—it is
A well-lit afternoon
                but the lights go on
& you know I'm there.
                    Back in those previous frames
Is a walk through a town.
                    It sobers you up
To dance like that. Extraordinary to dance
Like that. Ordinarily, can be seen, dancing
In the streets. Ah, well, thanks for the shoes, god
Like Goethe on his divan at Weimar, I'm wearing them
        on my right feet!

L. G. T. T. H.

Queen Victoria dove headfirst into the swimming pool,
      which was filled with blue milk.
I used to be baboons, but now I am person.
I used to be secretary to an eminent brain surgeon, but now I am
      quite ordinary. Oops! I've spilled the beans!
I wish mountains could be more appealing to the eye.
I wash sometimes. Meanwhile
Two-ton Tony Galento began to rub beef gravy over his entire body.
I wish you were more here.
I used to be Millicent, but now I am Franny.
I used to be a bowl of black China tea, but now I am walking back
      to the green fields of the people's republic.
Herman Melville is elbowing his way through
      the stringbeans toward us.
Oscar Levant handed the blue pill to Oscar Wilde during
      during the fish course. Then he slapped him.
I used to be blue, but now I am pretty. I wish broken bad person.
I wish not to see you tonight.
I wish to exchange this chemistry set for a goldfish please.
I used to be a little fairy, but now I am President
      of The United States.

IN BLOOD

"Old gods work"

"I gather up my tics & tilts, my stutters & imaginaries
            into the "up" leg
In this can-can. . ." "Are you my philosophy
If I love you, which I do. . ." "I want to know
It sensationally like the truth;" "I see in waves
Through you past me;" "But now I stop—" "I can love
What's for wear:" "But I dredge what I've bottomlessly canned
When I can't tell you . . ." "I love natural
Coffee beautifully . . ." "I'm conjugally love
Loose & tight in the same working" "I make myself
Feature by feature" "The angel from which each thing is most
            itself, from each, each,"
"I know there's a faithful anonymous performance"
"I wish never to abandon you" "I me room he" to
"Burn! this is not negligible, being poetic, & not feeble!"

PEKING

These are the very rich garments of the poor
Tousling gradations of rainbow, song & soothing tricks
With a crooked margin there & there is here: we
Are the waiting fragments of his sky, bouncing
            a red rubber ball in the veins.

Do you have a will? And one existing so forgets all
Desuetude desultory having to move again, take power from snow,
Evening out not more mild than beastly kind, into a symbol.
I hate that. I think the couple to be smiles over glasses, and

Questions not to find you, the which they have. O Marriage
Talking as you is like talking for a computer, needing to be
Abacus, adding machine, me. Up from the cave's belly, down
            from the airy populace
That lace my soul, a few tears from the last the sole surviving
            Texas Ranger,

Freed, freely merge with your air, dance. Blue are its snowflakes
Besprinkled blue lights on his eyes, & flakes. For her

I'd gladly let the snake wait under my back, and think, to walk,
And pass our long love's day. Landscape rushing away.

SOVIET SOUVENIR

What strikes the eye hurts, what one hears is a lie.
The river is flowing again between its banks.
Grant one more summer, O you Gods! that once I did not ask
The windows through which the bells toll are like doors

Because she is direct in her actions and in her feelings
Under the puns of the troop, there are frescoes
On the rudder, which you set against a bracelet's fire, and
Which goes toward you with each beat.

I find myself there; am I finally ill at ease with my own
Principle? Fortune be praised! Immense density, not divinely,
              bathes us
I hear walking in my legs
The savage eyes into wood look for the head they can live in

It's my window, even now, around me, full of darkness, dumb,
              so great!
My heart willingly again beginning crying out; and at the same time
              anxious, love, to contain.

SO GOING AROUND CITIES

to Doug & Jan Oliver

"I order you operate. I was not made to suffer."
Probing for old wills, and friendships, for to free
to New York City, to be in History, New York City being
History at that time." "And I traded my nights
for Intensity; & I barter my right to Gold; & I'd traded
my eyes much earlier, when I was circa say seven years old
for ears to hear Who was speaking, & just exactly who
was being told . . . ." & I'm glad
    I hear your words so clearly
    & I would not have done it
      differently
    & I'm amused at such simplicity, even so,
inside each & every door. And now I'm with you, instantly,
& I'll see you tomorrow night, and I see you constantly, hopefully
though one or the other of us is often, to the body-mind's own self
more or less out of sight! Taking walks down any street, High
Street, Main Street, walk past my doors! Newtown; Nymph Rd
    (on the Mesa); Waveland
Meeting House Lane, in old Southampton; or BelleVue Road
    in England, etcetera
Other roads; Manhattan; see them there where open or shut up behind
    "I've traded sweet times for answers. . ."
"They don't serve me anymore." They still serve me on the floor.
    Or,
as now, as floor. Now we look out the windows, go in &
    out the doors. The Door.
(That front door which was but & then at that time My door).
    I closed it
On the wooing of Helen. "And so we left schools for her." For
She is not one bit fiction; & she is easy to see;
    & she leaves me small room
For contradiction. And she is not alone; & she is not one bit
    lonely in the large high room, &
invention is just vanity, which is plain. She
is the heart's own body, the body's own mind in itself
    self-contained.
& she talks like you; & she has created truly not single-handedly
Our tragic thing, America. And though I would be I am not afraid

of her, & you also not. You, yourself, I,
Me, myself, me. And no, we certainly have not pulled down
        our vanity: but
We wear it lightly here,
                here where I traded evenly,
                                & even gladly
health, for sanity; here
                where we live day-by-day
                                on the same spot.
My English friends, whom I love & miss, we talk to ourselves here,
        & we two
rarely fail to remember, although we write seldom, & so must seem
        gone forever.
In the stained sky over this morning the clouds seem about to burst.
        What is being remembering
Is how we are, together. Like you we are always bothered, except
        by the worst; & we are living
        as with you we also were
fired, only, mostly, by changes in the weather. For Oh dear hearts,
When precious baby blows her fuse / it's just our way
        of keeping amused.
That we offer of & as excuse. Here's to you. All the very best.
        What's your pleasure? Cheers.

PICNIC

The dancer grins at the ground.
The mildest of alchemists will save him.
(Note random hill of chairs). & he will prove
       useful to her in time,
the ground to be their floor.

      like pennies to a three year old,
      like a novel, the right novel, to a 12 year old,
      like a 39 Ford to a Highschool kid
      like a woman is to a man, a girl
          who is a woman
              is her self's own soul
              and her man is himself
                   his own
                     & whole.

ADDENDA

    & I can't buy
          with submission
    & tho I feel often
           & why not
battered,
      I can't be beaten.
  But I have been eaten, 7 times
      by myself
& I go my way, by myself, I being
by myself only when useful, as, for example,
    you are to me now,
        to you.

XXXIV

Time flies by like a great whale
And I find my hand grown stale at the throttle
Of my many faceted and fake appearance
Who bucks and spouts by detour under the sheets
Hollow portals of solid appearance
Movies are poems, a holy bible, the great mother to us
People go by in the fragrant day
Accelerate softly my blood
But blood is still blood and tall as a mountain blood
Behind me green rubber grows, feet walk
In wet water, and dusty heads grow wide
Padre, Father, or fat old man, as you will,
I am afraid to succeed, afraid to fail
Tell me now, again, who I am

LXXXI

Musick strides through these poems
just as it strides through me! The red block
Dream of Hans Hoffman keeps going away and
Coming back to me.   He is not "The Poems."
        (my dream a drink with Lonnie Johnson we
discuss the code of the west)
                        How strange to be gone in a minute!
too soon for the broken arm. Ripeness begins corrupting every tree
Each strong morning   in air we get our feet wet
                                (my dream
a crumpled horn)   it hurts.   Huddie Ledbetter is dead
whose grief I would most assuage   Sing I must   and with Music
        I must rage
Against those whose griefs I would most assuage   (my dream
"DEAR CHRIS, hello. It is 5:15 a.m.

LXVII

(clarity! clarity!) a semblance of motion, omniscience.
There is no such thing as a breakdown
To cover the tracks of "The Hammer"   (the morning sky
gets blue and red and I get worried about
mountains of mounting pressure
and the rust on the bolts in my door
Some kind of Bowery Santa Claus   I wonder
down the secret streets of Roaring Gap
A glass of chocolate milk, head of lettuce, dark-
Bearden is dead. Chris is dead. Jacques Villon is dead.
Patsy awakens in heat and ready to squabble
I wonder if people talk about me *secretly*? I wonder if I'm
      fooling myself
about pills? I wonder what's in the icebox? out we go
to the looney movie   & the grace of the make-believe bed

LXV

Dreams, aspirations of presence! Innocence gleaned,
annealed! The world in its mysteries are explained,
and the struggles of babies congeal. A hard core is formed.
Today I thought about all those radio waves
He eats of the fruits of the great Speckle bird,
Pissing on the grass!
I too am reading the technical journals,
Rivers of annoyance undermine the arrangements
Some one said "Blake-blues" and someone else "pill-head"
Meaning bloodhounds.
Washed by Joe's throbbing hands
She is introspection.
It is a Chinese signal.
There is no such thing as a breakdown

LVI

banging around in a cigarette   she isn't "in love"
She murmurs of signs to her fingers
in my paintings for they are present
The withered leaves fly higher than dolls can see
What thwarts this fear I love
Mud on the first day (night, rather
gray his head goes   his feet green
Frances Marion nudges himself gently into the big blue sky
Joyful ants nest on the roof of my tree
I like to beat people up.
Summer so histrionic, marvelous dirty days
It is a human universe: & I
sings like Casals in furtive dark July; Out we go
to the looney movie   to the make believe bed

"DEAR CHRIS

it is 3:17 a.m. in New York city, yes, it is
1962, it is the year of parrot fever. In
Brandenburg, and by the granite gates, the
old come-all-ye's streel into the street. Yes, it is now,
the season of delight. I am writing to you to say that
I have gone mad. Now I am sowing the seeds which shall,
when ripe, master the day, and
portion out the night. Be watching for me when blood
flows down the streets. Pineapples are a sign
that I am coming. My darling, it is nearly time. Dress
the snowman in the Easter sonnet we made for him
when scissors were in style. For now, goodbye, and
all my love, The Snake"

THE COMPLETE PRELUDE: Title Not Yet Fixed Upon

for Clark

Upon the river, point me out my course
That blows from the green fields and from the clouds
And from the sky: be nothing better
Than a wandering cloud
Come fast upon me
Such as were not made for me.
I cannot miss my way. I breathe again
That burthen of my own natural self
The heavy weight of many a weary day
Coming from a house
Shall be my harbour; promises of human life
Are mine in prospect;
Now I am free, enfranchis'd and at large.
The earth is all before me: with a heart

& the result was elevating thoughts
Among new objects simplified, arranged
And out of what had been, what was, the place
'O'er the blue firmament a radiant white,'
Was thronged with impregnations, like those wilds
That into music touch the passing wind,
Had been inspired, and walk'd about in dreams,
And in Eclipse, my meditations turn'd
And unencroached upon, now, seemed brighter far
Though fallen from bliss, a solitary, full of caverns, rocks
And audible seclusions; here also found an element that pleased her
Tried her strength; made it live. Here
Neither guilt, nor vice; nor misery forced upon my sight
Could overthrow my trust in Courage, Tenderness, & Grace.
In the tender scenes I most did take my delight.

Thus strangely did I war against myself
What then remained in such Eclipse? what light
The wizard instantaneously dissolves
Through all the habitations of past years
And those to come, and hence an emptiness
& shall continue evermore to make

& shall perform to exalt and to refine
Inspired, celestial presence ever pure
From all the sources of her former strength.
Then I said: 'and these were mine,
Not a deaf echo, merely, of the thought
But living sounds. Yea, even the visible universe
                was scann'd
And, as by the simple waving of a wand
With something of a kindred spirit, fell
Beneath the domination of a taste
Its animation and its deeper sway.'

BOULDER

Up a hill, short
of breath , then breathing

up stairs, & down, & up, & down again

to

NOISE

Your warm powerful Helloes
friends,
still slightly breathless

in
a three-way street
hug

Outside

& we can move
& we move   Inside

to STARBURSTS   of Noise!

The human voice is how.

Lewis's, boyish & clear;   & Allen's, which persists,

& His,   & Hers,   & All of them thems!

& then
Anne's, once again, (and as I am)   "Ted!"

Then

O, Lady!,   O, See, among all things which exist

O this!, this breathing, we.

WHERE THE CEILING LIGHT BURNS

Since we had changed
The smell of snow, stinging in nostrils as the wind lifts it
      from a beach
Today a hockey coach died in
The green of days: the chimneys
Morning again, nothing has to be done,
          maybe buy a piano or make fudge
Totally abashed & smiling

                    I walk in
                    sit down and
                    face the frigidaire
You say that everything is very simple and interesting
'the picturesque
common lot'   the unwarranted light
the fever & obscurity of your organisms
on what grounds shall we criticize the City Manager?

CLASH BY NIGHT

You still smell
   of disinfectant. A fellow
      like you
gotta make a stand somewhere
      I guess.
      He was one
of the last of the Western bandits.
       Gets into scrapes.
Got Life.
    Spends most of it in jail.
       Do you ever fish?
I just go down & look at the water.
      Pretty, ain't it?
Is it?
   It's a Carnival.
     A pig sty.
      Loop-de-loop.
No, it ain't pretty.
    Your kind
      drift from nowhere
to
  nowhere
    until they get close to you.
No telling what they'll do then.
      I need some shoes.

Other Yellow Press books:

15 Chicago Poets edited by Richard Friedman, Peter Kostakis, and
Darlene Pearlstein

ISBN 0-916328-03-1 (paperback) $3.00
ISBN 0-916328-04-x (cloth) $7.95

Alice Ordered Me To Be Made — Poems 1975 by Alice Notley

ISBN 0-916328-02-3 (paperback) $2.50
ISBN 0-916328-06-6 (cloth) $6.95

Straight — Poems 1971-1975 by Richard Friedman

ISBN 0-916328-00-7 (paperback) $2.00

Yellow Press Books are distributed by Serendipity Books
1790 Shattuck Avenue, Berkeley Ca. 94709
Please order from them

Typeset by Barrett Watten at The West Coast Print Center
in California Medium and Italic. 26 cloth bound books are
lettered A-Z and signed with a holograph poem by Ted Berrigan.
3 cloth bound books are hors commerce and numbered 1, 2, 3.